Starlings

For Pandelis & Julia,

"Still getting lost nonetheless"

Yours,

ELIOT CARDINAUX

Eliot Cardinaux

THE BODILY PRESS
Amherst, MA

Starlings

Copyright © 2025 Eliot Cardinaux

All rights reserved. Except for brief passages quoted for usage in online or print sources (e.g. newspaper, magazine, podcast), no part of this book may be reproduced in any form or by any means, electronic or mechanical, including photocopying and recording, or by any information storage and retrieval system, without permission in writing from the publisher.

This book is set in Cardo and Garamond Premier Pro.
Book design and layout by Eliot Cardinaux.
eliotcardinaux.com

Cover image:
Tasha Robbins, *Starlings*, 2024
Acrylic/Found cardboard,
8⅞ x 9" (22.8 x 22.5 cm)
All Rights Reserved
Copyright © 2024 Tasha Robbins

Bodily Press logo designed by Katya Popova.
popova.space

THE BODILY PRESS
www.bodilypress.com
@thebodilypress

Starlings

Also by Eliot Cardinaux

Poetry & Chapbooks

On the Long Blue Night
Quiet Labor
Toy Elegy
This Music From Another Room
Island
Rope of Sand
The Ocean from Here to Here
Blue Flowers for Michael Palmer
Wandering Subject

Music

No Dreams Here
Gestures: Schaatsen (with Flin van Hemmen)
American Thicket (with Mat Maneri, Flin van Hemmen,
 & Thomas Morgan)
Sweet Beyond Witness
Odysseus Alone (with Kresten Osgood & Thomas Morgan)
Take Me by the Hand of Darkness (with Will McEvoy
 & Max Goldman)
A Living Past (with Jonas Engel, Asger Thomsen,
 & Simon Forchhammer)
What the Wildflower Witnessed (with Our Hearts as Thieves)
Pavane (with Gary Fieldman)
Out of Our Systems (with Will McEvoy & Max Goldman)
Pain is a Form of Violence Prone to Happiness
 (with Our Hearts as Thieves)
Imminence (with Gary Fieldman)
The Rock Beneath the Tree (with Bram Kincheloe)

in memory of Pierre Joris

Poems are paradoxes. Paradoxical is the rhyme, that gathers sense and sense, sense and countersense: a chance meeting at a place in language-time nobody can foresee, it lets this word coincide with that other one — for how long? For a limited time: the poet, who wants to stay true to that principle of freedom that announces itself in the rhyme, now has to turn his back to the rhyme. Away from the border — or across it, off into the borderless!

—Paul Celan, *Microliths* (translation, Pierre Joris)

A sign of estrangement, to poetize or sing is to risk irrelevance, to be haunted by poetry's or music's possible irrelevance ("Tell it to the birds"), but nothing could be more relevant than estrangement.

—Nathaniel Mackey, *Splay Anthem* (introduction)

Table of Contents

STARLINGS

XI. / 15
XII. / 16
XIII. / 18
XIV. / 20
XV. / 21

LANGUAGE, I FEEL AT ELSE HERE

Mile Forty-Eight / 25
Mile Forty-Nine / 26
Mile Fifty / 27
Mile Fifty-One / 28
Mile Fifty-Two / 29
Mile Fifty-Three / 30
Mile Fifty-Four / 31
Mile Fifty-Five / 32
Mile Fifty-Six / 33
Mile Fifty-Seven / 34
Mile Fifty-Eight / 35
Mile Fifty-Nine / 36

CLOSED CAPTIONS

XVI. / 39
XVII. / 40
XVIII. / 41
XIX. / 42
XX. / 43

THE RESISTANT STATE

Mile Sixty / 47
Mile Sixty-One / 48
Mile Sixty-Two / 49
Mile Sixty-Three / 50
Mile Sixty-Four / 51
Mile Sixty-Five / 52
Mile Sixty-Six / 53
Mile Sixty-Seven / 54
Mile Sixty-Eight / 55
Mile Sixty-Nine / 56
Mile Seventy / 57
Mile Seventy-One / 58

THE CONNOTED BODY

XXI. / 61
XXII. / 62
XXIII. / 63
XXIV. / 64
XXV. / 66

◊

Acknowledgments / 69

Notes / 71

About the Author / 83

STARLINGS

XI.

for Jesper Zeuthen

& the trumpet
your voice reached across centuries
the unadorned melody   electrical box
a pigeon's nest   my name
not here   not now
& setting down roots in the past
the present   bright major

the horns sing   *here I go again*
& all this is cogent in ensemble
to know I am capable
is to know what I'm capable
of   threading the needle
of isolation into the dream

this place looks smaller
without smoke in the air
here I go now
rise & be subsumed

XII.

for Michael Rexen

red-lit & curtained into
patience   you turn the wheel
despite your preference
on the edge of life

they burn it down & you
rebuild   revealing bridges
there where the carrier pylon
should stand   a distance
from East to West   where
the people are not at war

you built   your instrument
on the road through sick Europe
begging
just because we got paid
that we not settle
playing for ourselves
singing
that to love is better
than to profess

your country shares
my grandfather's name
entertainment bores you
respect your audience
you said   *I want it*
to be generous
evidence enough
of this gentle thing

XIII.

for Michaela Turcerová

change   time passing
another instrument
thinking for itself
an eagle of air
between mourning & comfort
towing behind itself
for all our sorrows
what has been believed
what has been   believed in

the effort of six musicians
becomes the effort of bridges
straining   bridges in the air
the distances
I & you   surveying
the difference

to experience wonder
speechless   underlying itself
being named   *surround & destroy*
regardless of disbelief

the universe fails   the forest
waking up   *don't take*
the obvious road   it's time
for coffee   put on a record
read the news   dawn chorus
accept what comes   *the power*
of beauty   to right all wrongs

XIV.

a performer eating
microphones   enters
the posthuman age
enters the institution
admitted
for sanity

no adequate destination
continue to wander   pick up
the cigarette butts   go home
where is home   my heart
is in my chest   America

renew another passport
enter the password   *debasement*
follow the accusations
back to the source
the people are not at war
yet   the sun is cold in the sky

XV.

for Shana Bulhan

the anonymous icons
of your collage   in their architectural
surround   me in my seat
on the plane   back
to the bughouse   king at the center
an immediate threat
in this random position
no longer torn   frayed edges
that never fit   but perhaps this time

standing out   in the rain
a motherly figure   hanging
over me   her initials a memory of
who I am   it is needed
this ride on the Pike

a pike's bones are thin
lodged in the throat like
language   words
are not things   a lemon
never   really a lemon
fishing

the state's first letter
capital   the call
to be revolutionary   protesters
threatened   with broken bones
for not bending   to university
complicity
& the wisdom   to know
the difference

standing in   four inch
melted snow   old snow
from Copenhagen home
this old road well-rutted
still getting lost nonetheless

LANGUAGE, I FEEL AT ELSE HERE

Mile Forty-Eight

Don't stop thinking
about tomorrow

or you'll grieve.
Lay down in

discomfortable
structure, jockey

for a little solitude,
sleep, underrated

in fetal position,
come to terms.

Things cannot
shake their names.

Mile Forty-Nine

Language, I feel
at else here. This

leap into normalcy,
all scurry toward

our summation. We
found you & named

ourselves *people*,
a catachresis.

This is where
I find myself

in love, in you,
& everywhere.

Mile Fifty

Interpellation:
to refurbish,

alter, or falsify
a public

answer, arresting
ourselves unfinished.

I'd rather open
onto the real con-

flagration held
at a distance,

inhabit each
other, resisting

settlement
with you.

The note is
a monad, no-

madic collapse
of percussion

breaking on
my tongue.

Mile Fifty-One

Never
at the outset

of anything
threatened

the squeeze
of sub-zero

air. The state
of our love

defined as
such that we

could not find
it, whether un–

ified or nu–
merously so,

still knowing
it was there,

stateless, as
it were.

Mile Fifty-Two

Honest, I can-
not see you.

Lift me out
of yourself

to hold. I am
not here to

argue the serene
expanse of distance

squirming out of
your trembling

hands. To be
in love & to love

enaction just as
much as essence.

Look toward
the wavering.

Mile Fifty-Three

The room rearranged,
mimed in memory.

A trace of coolness,
gift left high

above the bed
this life ago. &

why should I
remember? Pain

of pleasure gone.
Scarce resource,

love, what can
I give?

Mile Fifty-Four

for Mat Maneri

Exquisite
agony, *dal*

niente,
a thread

from silence.
Is your head

bowed, learning
one mother tongue

in the void of
another,

waiting on
a secret?

Mile Fifty-Five

Desolation. Melody.
Negation inheriting

all imperative.
A slow pulse toward

the naming
of things as they pass

to shoulder you.
A smile in a smile.

Wide recognition.
A sudden loneliness.

Alone at the break
of things, their breaking

done to oneself & to
others along the way.

Mile Fifty-Six

for Joseph Donahue

Is envy hell?
Or is it

the uninterrupted
stream of eternity

tying us to gravity
& the earth that causes us

to envy
even the life of it?

The lived life, living,
not this

fragment as a whole.
A hole is an envy, too

for what goes in,
arises out of it, no-

thing an arrival
we can name.

Mile Fifty-Seven

Did I secretly like it?
My system, flooded

with air on the Ama-
brogade. What is it

to return? I walk so
briefly through the

memory on my way,
& everywhere a trigger

comes to my mind.
I hold it at a distance.

Shudder. Sometimes
I smile uncontrollably.

Mile Fifty-Eight

Tread lightly around
my body, falling

into it. Our senses
merged. To lay

down in heightened
pitch, where harmony

wears thin. The lines
that pull against

the gravity of
our love. With-

drawing long enough to
stay. A single syllable.

Mile Fifty-Nine

To be
this kernel shelled

in anonymity,
all dissonant surround

gathered in weight-
less resolve

to dissipate.
A simultaneous

undoing. Who,
in the world, am I?

CLOSED CAPTIONS

XVI.

for Michael Tillyer

our labor an exploit of desolate beauty
strange & horrible days   in history
bright with music   a world premier
fill the house   unheated
for lack of entry   a cycle
completed   is never
completed   drag yourself along
singing   *in the loop & out*

poetry is   the language that otherwise
slips through the cracks   holding
onto your pieces   twirling
the queen   around your thumb
stepping onto the last
public square

we will walk the savage earth
together   see the lights
of the city   poetry is
everywhere   it has emerged

XVII.

for Matthew Shipp

unfinished edges   surface
pierced by walls of music
mystery   touch & tone
inquisitive to pounding
soft compulsion   tense
in the jaw   full body

don't ask
too many questions
dynamics can articulate
& argue their way
through light

gather sense & sense
within a field   a calm
bright pain   *that beauty*
all of it   & faith
enough to carry
more than to hold

not you   the forsaken
trying to forsake
the forsaking
your dancing
shoulders   life & death
in between   *keep moving*

XVIII.

you mumbled   *I love you*
for me to remember
what I could not hear
slant sunlight   in winter
rhyming   invisible rise
out of time's noise
in kindness   the threat
of all murderous ways
perceived

first spring day before
the operation   on an excursion
from home   whipped through
with alcohol   years ago
we got pulled over
on this road   you & I
but we hadn't been drinking
[industrial noise]

inconclusive   arrival
questions   sing largely
of nothing   strong coffee
to wake the day   assemble
furniture   closed captions
a sign of life

XIX.

for Tasha Robbins

alpha   bet   two steps
to leave your house   Celanian
dust on my wings   a pack
of letters left behind   don't need
an excuse to wander
back to you   but still

playing ping pong with
my mind   *aleph   beit*
each unit   structure
for a revolution   shall we
sing   *Cantarnos*
on the box again

they *did it & did it & did it*
to us all   now what
since the box is open
who put the money in

XX.

for Andrew Mossin

twilight   encroaching pain
turn the corner   sunlight
stretches the real   over several blocks
sacred music sways   the heads of a crowd
in green   eerie light   staid silence
broken bottles on a sidewalk
the enemy is closer to each other's throats

make way for endless marching
down a dead end road   spring is coming
too   geese flock down the page
murmurations   suspended
moments   in time   for beauty
a sensitive way

to translate what is good
into language   out of language
out of this world's attachments
the storm unhinged   a floating
door   past the flickering film
unfolding outside   leaving us stunned at each
private threshold   the twilight's witnesses
gazing further in

THE RESISTANT STATE

Mile Sixty

for Asger Thomsen

The drone's note
a hinge then

a fracture,
echoed in

anxious flutter,
insistence forcing

our exhaustively
collective hand.

The air goes out.
Sun needs

no definition
unless it can't

be found. My
Danish notebook

open on my leg,
betraying all

selfhood. Is it
fair to question?

Mile Sixty-One

To tremble
with fear &

anger, enter
into the poetic

headspace, small
door above

the fridge. Turn on
the oven, categorize

all meaning, state
the obvious elan,

drape & fixture,
before the house.

Mile Sixty-Two

for Katya Popova

These snowflakes
come together,

bury us in white
whose beauty

is desolate labor.
A definite space

to fill. Slow down
in the music. Reach

the murmuring wall.
Diverge. Divest. Distill.

Collapse the formulaic.
Evaporate the obvious.

Let the inevitable rise
wash over you.

Mile Sixty-Three

to the memory of René Char

What came before
never came to be

because we saw it
from here. Spring

inklings of death,
what horizons ex-

tend that way, be-
yond humankind?

Dissent, as brute &
bravery disentangle,

recognize yourself
in the gut's mirror.

Mile Sixty-Four

in memory of Pierre Joris

In my gut I feel —
not something

that is missing,
something that

is lost. What is
lost can be found,

in the language
behind language.

This is how it works
driving over a creek

bed, or writing
to the dead.

Mile Sixty-Five

To enter the resistant
state. Inhabit the under-

spoken. Travel at a stand-
still. Counter the route.

To baffle speech, what-
ever project. Empire

into nausea on its heels
the impaled imperative.

Mile Sixty-Six

for Niamh Timmons

So much time spent
addressing language.

Metamorphose, feeding
two seeds to one bird

& your tongue will follow.
Agency rolls off the tongue

like a pill. Stoop down
or the dog will eat it.

Mile Sixty-Seven

Decathexis, run off
in rivulets to bliss.

Is it eternity, is it
a paper ending?

Blood, lighten
my head where

anticipation grave-
ly detaches. Grieve

a projected else-
where I am staying.

Mile Sixty-Eight

Song-singers,
broken above

the river, all
in pieces, can

you forget
each instant,

formulation,
form, formation,

difference the eye
cannot follow,

blended into nu-
merous one? I was

that wish in the sky
there, above the road.

Mile Sixty-Nine

in memory of Daniel Levine

Here you are, the age
you promised never

to be. This book is
probably shy of you.

To count out your
running, & mine.

Mile Seventy

Enamor dread,
the phlegmatic

clearing. Wilder-
ness, I come to

on my own, wake
with the first word,

native to elsewhere.
Can I speak?

Mile Seventy-One

for Jade Welch

Stable, I feel
& fear for you.

We are not inured
to your injured

urgency. The long
arc of unkindness

circles me. To
ravage & rebuild.

THE CONNOTED BODY

For Mireille Gansel

*Mireille, pour l'instant je prends des risques.
Plus tard, je reviendrai sur ce site où des langues
natales se croisent et croissent comme des racines,
je vous le promets. Sous le signe de Pierre.*

XXI.

for Bei Dao,
at a distance

effort   exhaustion
sunlight   making its way
through the body   oxycodone
fading   moving like a sloth
not to wake the pain

resisting   history as poetry
to achieve some innocence
a world that is just   in fiction
is just in the world   vignettes of your childhood
famine colored by pagoda blossoms
white rabbit candy   will I ever
understand   what is left of that world
between self   & other   a lover's
vulnerable blessing

lay down & read   between the books
a thread of dreaming   sewn into habitation
worn out with desire to write   to cross the road
lifted up by a stranger   waking

XXII.

for & with Jo Ianni

have you misheard   the connoted body
how many mosques for Notre Dame to burn
satisfactory   systems of value
judgement   I think of choices
mere facts that exist   the terrific
terrors   that water constitutes
experience   & air

I think of you Jo   the inexplicable
replaced   by the inexcusable
the world can be just if we let it
remember   to remind each
other   sew the limbs back
on

that was only two buildings
my grandmother said   after 9/11
that harshness has a place if there's heart in it
you said   her brother's heart beating
out of my chest   a child's fantasy   *reality*
out of this world's distortions
searched for & won

XXIII.

for Mark Scroggins

each star links the wide occult
brim of the dipper   *Americana
Arcana*   foolishly in synch
with the spray of bullets
shattering bottles   no one
will ever pay for   glass in the dirt
glass in the land   a name
a name misspoken   *a catachresis
at the origin*   takes root   says
you're welcome for my means

irony   all of a sudden
takes hold   loose shirts to protest
the overdevelopment
of crisis   torn in annoyance
& horror   spring break-
ing through the evening   chill
before sundown   *twilight
of freedom*   brothers
am I one of you
at all

in the microtonal
hum   break the poem into pieces
I offer you spare parts   all I have
are fractures   the memories
must be dug out of the cracks

XXIV.

for Mireille Gansel

my beloved asks
what is the valence of desire
I ask you   *what is the valence
of despair*   a leaf   treeless
wanhope

if trees connote silence   life force
a bridge between them   mended
& rebuilt so many times   like a ship
of Theseus

will the wounds come to you seeking
lost homes in language   *the long, slow
movement of the flocks*   how
will you help the word to pass
to cross the river

root systems   rhizomes   site
of the Southern liberation   nodes
& internodes   the interstitial shock
of your revelation   land between native
tongues   *the underground springs
of a people's hinterland*
your translator's choice of words
in order to flower into language
must be laid bare

a branch with green leaves
carried out of a prison cell
in Vietnam
the poems etched with a pin
a cough   that shatters
breathless poetry   scolding
the silence surrounding
so many lines you carried
off into the borderless

is it still okay to ask when things
perhaps by now   have already begun
to come to pass
where the stigma of autumn burns
will anyone find these words
insensitive   trees
connote life   & silence
so many things that are said

XXV.

the only thing sure
is the fracture of myriad
futures   too early to tell
your fate   but was it
vanity   to have hoped for
meaning   a ludicrous project
from the true opponent   a limitless
courage flows into you   whether
illness or enemy appears
in the flesh

the apocalyptic   present
throughout history   is not a given
it has to be searched for & won   that this
is reality   fighting is an act
an effort   not a sign of giving up
or giving in   *thank you for sharing*
the burden of hope with us   hope
is a cruel thing   not the opposite
of despair   it's harder
to hope   I think

invasive bird   why do you mock me
so   sing my melody back to me
make shapes of your numerous
self   enclosed   in language
changeling   released into Central
Park because Shakespeare
mentioned you   *starling*
though you are so beautiful
still   don't despair
my star   *they destroy*
while we want to live

Acknowledgments

My sincere thanks to David Need, the editor of *Middlelost*, for publishing poems "XI"-"XX" therein.

The two long poems in this book are continuations of the work begun in "Rope of Sand" from *The Ocean from Here to Here* (Bodily Press, 2025) and in "Black Swans" and "Your Song Cast Out on the Wilderness" from *Wandering Subject* (Bodily Press, 2025).

"Mile Sixty" appears on the cover of the album *Rhizom* by Asger Thomsen (Gotta Let It Out, Copenhagen, 2025).

"XXIV" & "XXV" appeared in *Fortnightly Review*. My thanks to Robert Archambeau.

My deepest love and thanks to my life partner Shana Bulhan, who, in typical fashion, observed the tendency of these poems with unique accuracy, describing them as "murmurations," thus giving me the title, *Starlings*. Shana inhabits these pages as much as I do, not only in their love and support, but in their constant and ever-present insight into the poetics and craft inherent to what I am trying to do.

Thank you to Tasha Robbins for collaborating with me on the cover of this collection, which is graced by her wonderful painting of starlings in their sacred and not-so-native habitat.

Love and thanks to Jo Ianni for our continued exchange.

Profound thanks to both Aldon Nielsen and John Phillips for being such attuned first readers of this work.

Thank you to Asger Thomsen, Jesper Løvdal, Mads Egetoft, Hein Westgaard, Margaux Oswald, Michaela Turcerová, and to all my friends in Denmark who helped make this work possible.

A very special thank you to Mireille Gansel for her friendship and correspondence, and for encouraging my own humble efforts toward the transhumance of the poetic word.

Thank you to Michael Rexen for his immediate kinship, and for the music he so generously shares.

Thank you to Kresten Osgood, my oldest friend in Denmark, for never giving up on my art.

Thank you to Katya Popova for offering me a place to land.

Thank you to Niamh Timmons for their friendship, kindness, support, and constant care.

Thank you to Deja Carr for her camaraderie and for carrying her own music and poetry with such grace.

Lastly, an enormous thank you to Michael Tillyer and Susan Foley for providing an enduring backdrop for my music and poetry at NEVAmuseum and Anchor House of Artists in Northampton, Massachusetts to this day.

Notes

The epigraphs at the beginning of this collection are taken from Paul Celan's *Microliths They Are, Little Stones: Posthumous Prose*, translated by Pierre Joris (Contra Mundum Press, 2020), and from Nathaniel Mackey's introduction to *Splay Anthem* (New Directions, 2006).

Starlings

"XI" was written at a performance by Danish alto saxophonist/composer/bandleader Jesper Zeuthen's Empty Pocket Sextet at Christiania Jazz Club, Copenhagen, Denmark, February, 2025.

"XII" was written at a solo performance by Omani-Danish musician and instrument builder Michael Rexen at Koncertkirken, Copenhagen, Denmark, February, 2025. The phrase *"there where the carrier pylon / should stand"* is derived from a fragment in Paul Celan's *Microliths* (Contra Mundum).

"XIII" was written at the premier of Danish composer Pauline Hogstrand's sextet for mixed strings, woodwinds, and laptop, "Eagle of Air," which took place at Koncertkirken, Copenhagen, Denmark, February, 2025. The lines *"the power / of beauty / to right all wrongs"* are taken from William Carlos Williams' poem "To a Dog Injured in the Street," collected in *The William Carlos Williams Reader* (J. Laughlin, 1966). The lines refer to WCW's kinship with the French Resistance poet René Char.

"XIV" calls up the line "Debasement is the password of the base" from Bei Dao's poem "The Answer," collected in *The August Sleepwalker*, translation Bonnie S. McDougall (New Directions, 1990).

Language, I Feel at Else Here

"Mile Fifty-Six" calls up "The Land that Secretes Light," Dan Beachy-Quick's review of Joseph Donahue's *Terra Lucida XIII–XXI* in *The Los Angeles Review of Books*, January 24, 2025.

Closed Captions

In "XVI," the line "*in the loop & out*" is the opening lyric from the author's composition "Disillusionment," sung and recorded on *A Living Past* (Bodily Press, 2020).

◇

"XVII" was written at a solo performance by pianist Matthew Shipp at the Northampton Center for the Arts (MA), February, 2025. The line "*gather sense & sense*" is taken from the epigraph by Paul Celan that appears at the beginning of this collection.

The lines "*that beauty / all of it*" refer loosely to a phrase from James Baldwin's essay "Down at the Cross: Letter from a Region in my Mind," collected in *The Fire Next Time* (Dial Press, 1963/ Knopf Doubleday, 1992). Baldwin's phrase reads:

"When I was very young, and was dealing with my buddies in those wine- and urine-stained hallways, something in me wondered, What will happen to all that beauty?"

The closing lines in "XVII" are taken from a poem by Pierre Joris: "not to worry: / you had your birth / given you [/] you / will be / given your death — // in between / keep moving" from *In Between Keep Moving: A Pierre Joris Reader*, edited by Ariel Resnikoff & Pierre Joris (Contra Mundum, TBA).

◊

"XIX" was written after leaving the studio of the painter-among-poets Tasha Robbins, where she and the author had been working toward the publication of *An Angel Alphabet*, a book of Robbins' paintings visually depicting the Hebrew Alphabet Malachim in Cornelius Agrippa's Angelic Script.

In Arabic, *beit* is a house or a tent, also a metrical unit of poetry.

Also alluded to in this poem, *Unit Structures* is the name of a musical system devised by pianist Cecil Taylor, also the title of one of his albums (Blue Note, 1966).

Cantarnos is a composition by pianist Andrew Hill from the album *Black Fire* (Blue Note, 1964). The phrase "*did it & did it & did it*" is a nod to the drummer Roy Haynes.

In "XX," the phrase "*a sensitive way*" is derived from the title, *Sensible Wege*, of a book of poems by the East German poet Reiner Kunze, as written about by the French-Jewish poet and translator Mireille Gansel in her memoir and philosophical treatise, *Translation as Transhumance*, translated by Ros Schwartz (Feminist Press, 2017). The phrase "to translate what is good [...] out of language" is derived from a public discussion that took place between Gansel and Shoshana Olidort at Amherst College in March, 2025.

The Resistant State

"Mile Sixty" alludes to *The Danish Notebook* by Michael Palmer (Nightboat Books, 2023), also collected in *Active Boundaries* (New Directions, 2008). This poem, along with others in the collection, was written in Copenhagen, Denmark.

"Mile Sixty-Three" alludes to the poem "*Les Poumons*" ("The Lungs") by René Char, collected in *Le Marteau sans maître suivi de Moulin premier* (Gallimard, 2002). The poem's two lines read: "The appearance of a firearm / Recognition in the gut." (translation, Eliot Cardinaux).

"Mile Sixty-Four" alludes to the concept of a palimpsest, as it regards translation ("the language / behind language"), here again derived from the aforementioned public discussion that took place between Mireille Gansel and Shoshana Olidort at Amherst College in March, 2025.

"Mile Sixty-Nine" was written on what would have been the 40th birthday of the late trumpeter/composer Daniel Levine.

The Connoted Body

The dedication at the beginning of "The Connoted Body" translates, "Mireille, for now, I'm taking risks. Later, I'll return to this site where native tongues cross and extend themselves like roots, I promise. Under the sign of Pierre [Joris]."

"XXI" engages by turns with the Chinese exile-poet Bei Dao's memoir, *City Gate, Open Up*, translation Jeffrey Yang (New Directions, 2017), and with Marguerite Duras' novel *The Lover* (Knopf Doubleday, 2011). *Marguerite Duras: Worn Out with Desire to Write* is the title of a documentary on the life of Duras and the story behind *The Lover*, directed by Alan Benson and Daniel Wiles (Films Media Group, 1985).

◇

"XXII" was written in the midst of a text exchange with the poet Jo Ianni.

Given reference here, the phrase, "Reality is not. It has to be searched for and won" was written by Paul Celan, as translated by Pierre Joris and included in his essay "The Millennium Will Be Nomadic or It Will Not Be: Notes Towards a Nomadic Poetics (version 4.00)," collected in *A Nomad Poetics* (Wesleyan University Press, 2003).

Another reference to Celan occurs in the lines "remember / to remind each / other / sew the limbs back / on." In *Microliths* (Contra Mundum, 2020), Celan constructs the following thought: "Re-membering / also pre-membering, pre-thinking and storing of what could be" (translation, Pierre Joris).

Out of This World's Distortions is the title of an album by the trio Farmers by Nature (AUM Fidelity, 2011), comprised of pianist Craig Taborn, drummer Gerald Cleaver, and bassist William Parker.

◊

In "XXIII," the phrase "*American Arcana*" plays off the title of American poet Mark Scroggins' book of essays *Arcane Pleasures: On Poetry and Some Other Arts* (Three Count Pour, 2023).

The phrase "*a catachresis / at the origin*" is taken from the essay "Can the Subaltern Speak?" by South-Asian scholar, literary theorist, and feminist critic Gayatri Chakravorty Spivak, as collected in *Marxism and the Interpretation of Culture*, edited by Cary Nelson and Lawrence Grossberg (University of Illinois Press, 1988).

"The Twilight of Freedom" is the title of a poem by Stalin-era Russian poet Osip Mandelstam from his first collection, *Stone*, collected in *The Selected Poems of Osip Mandelstam*, Clarence Brown and W.S. Merwin, translators (NYRB, 2004).

Loosely referred to in this poem, "Fractured Memories" is a solo piano composition by the late trumpeter/composer Daniel Levine, recorded on the author's debut solo piano album *No Dreams Here* (self-released, 2014). A reference to this piece also occurs in "Black Swans," collected in *Wandering Subject* (Bodily Press, 2025).

◇

"XXIV" is written in direct response to several chapters in Mireille Gansel's *Translation as Transhumance* (Feminist Press, 2017). Those and other references are as follows.

The phrase "*what is the valence of desire*" is derived from the writings of South-Asian-American poet and scholar Shana Bulhan, also the author's romantic partner.

"A LEAF, treeless, for Bertold Brecht" is a poem by Paul Celan from *Schneepart* (*Snowpart*), collected in *Breathturn into Timestead: The Collected Later Poetry: A Bilingual Edition*, translated by Pierre Joris (FSG, 2014). The line "*so many things that are said*" is derived from Celan's poem, which itself is derived from Bertold Brecht's own poem "*An die Nachgeborenen*" ("To Those Born After").

Gansel, who worked closely with Brecht, refers to some lines in Brecht's poem, here translated by Ros Schwartz, in *Translation as Transhumance*: "What times are they, when / a talk about trees is almost a crime / because it implies silence about so many horrors?"

In her memoir, Gansel recounts reciting these lines of Brecht's to a Vietnamese friend at the site of the Southern liberation in Vietnam during the war, citing the link between trees, and silence in the face of atrocity, as it is evinced in Brecht's poem. She learns from her friend, however, that "for her people, the trees, the fragrance of the rice fields, of the flowers of the night, it was all part of the life forces, in no way different from commitment and resistance—quite the opposite" (*Translation as Transhumance*, pp. 52-53).

The lines "*the long, slow / movement of the flocks*" and "*the underground springs / of a people's hinterland*" are also taken from *Translation as Transhumance*, and refer more generally to the process of translation and trans-lingual poetics, from the translator's work, alongside native speakers, of tapping into the cultural wellsprings of a given language, to her equal task of shepherding the word across national, political, societal, and cultural borders.

The line "*a branch with green leaves*" refers directly to Gansel's encounter with the Vietnamese poet To Huu, who, while in prison, as she recounts on his behalf, had to resort to etching his poems onto the green leaves of a branch that was slipped into his cell by friends: "Those were my first publications, my first copies: branches, an entire branch, small, but with lots of leaves. That way, it's public. A branch . . . A branch with green leaves! It's innocent! Inoffensive! A branch that is both poetry and politics."

The line "*where the stigma of autumn burns*" is derived from a line by Reiner Kunze, also found in Gansel's *Translation as Transhumance*, therein translated by Ros Schwartz as "where the stigma(ta) of autumn burn(s)," with parentheses, presumably in order to convey Gansel's own openly undecided effort during the process of translation.

The line "*off into the borderless*" is taken from the epigraph at the beginning of this collection by Paul Celan.

It must be noted, again, that many of the insights that inform this poem were orally transmitted, and aurally absorbed during the aforementioned public discussion that took place between Mireille Gansel and Shoshana Olidort at Amherst College in March, 2025.

◇

In "XXV," the phrase "from the true opponent, a limitless courage flows into you" is taken from Franz Kafka's *The Zürau Aphorisms*, Roberto Calasso, editor (Random House, 2011).

The line "*thank you for sharing the burden of hope with us*" is a quote by Palestinian poet and exile Mahmoud Darwish, taken from the title essay in Bei Dao's collection, *Midnight's Gate*, Matthew Fryslie, translator; Christopher Mattison, editor (New Directions, 2005). The line "hope is a cruel thing" calls up Bei Dao's own poem, "Cruel Hope," from *The August Sleepwalker* (New Directions, 1990).

A note on the final stanza, addressed to the book's namesake:

An invasive species, European Starlings were first brought to America by Shakespeare enthusiasts who wanted for the "New World" to house every species of bird mentioned in Shakespeare's poetry and plays. The group released 100 starlings into Central Park in the 1890s (source: allaboutbirds.org). *Star*, German for "starling," was the name Wolfgang Amadeus Mozart gave to his own pet starling.

The lines *"they destroy / while we want to live"* were written by the Vietnamese poet Che Lan Vien, as quoted by Mireille Gansel, and translated into English by Ros Schwartz in Gansel's *Translation as Transhumance* (Feminist Press, 2017).

About the Author

ELIOT CARDINAUX is a poet, pianist, composer, publisher, and translator working at the edges of the lyric and improvised music. The author of *On the Long Blue Night* (Dos Madres, 2023), *Quiet Labor*, *Toy Elegy*, and *This Music From Another Room* (Bodily Press, 2024), *The Ocean from Here to Here* and *Wandering Subject* (Bodily Press, 2025), as well as numerous chapbooks, Eliot has also produced and appeared on over a dozen albums of original music, including *American Thicket* (Loyal Label, 2016), *Out of Our Systems* and *Pavane* (Bodily Press, 2022), and most recently *Imminence* (self-released, 2024) with USAmerican percussionist Gary Fieldman. He holds a bachelor's degree in contemporary improvisation from The New England Conservatory of Music, and an MFA in creative writing, with a focus on poetry, from the University of Massachusetts in Amherst. Eliot's poems and translations have appeared in *Jacket2*, *Meridian*, *Bennington Review*, *Tupelo Quarterly*, *California Quarterly*, *The Arts Fuse*, *Solstice*, *Spoon River Poetry Review*, and elsewhere. At present, he co-leads an American trio with bassist Will McEvoy and drummer Max Goldman, works in a duo with Gary Fieldman, leads his own Danish Quintet, and is a member of the international poetry and free-improvisation ensemble, Our Hearts as Thieves. He performs throughout Europe and the Northeastern United States He has taught literature and writing at UMass Amherst, and music as a postgraduate mentor at the Copenhagen Rhythmic Music Conservatory in Denmark. He works as a bookseller at Amherst Books, and as founding editor of The Bodily Press.

Author photograph by poet Shana Bulhan • shanabulhan.com

THE BODILY PRESS
bodilypress.bandcamp.com
www.bodilypress.com
@thebodilypress